Creative Thread Design

CREATIVE THREAD DESIGN

Mair Morris

B T Batsford Limited   London

Charles T Branford Company
Newton Centre   Massachusetts

© Mair Morris 1974
First published 1974
ISBN 0 7134 2783 3

Library of Congress Cataloguing in Publication Data
Morris, Mair
Creative Thread Design

1   Needlework.   2   Hand weaving.   1   Title.
TT750.M68   746.4   73-17334
ISBN 0-8231-7033-0

Designed by Libra Studios
Set in Monophoto Baskerville (169) 10 on 12 point
by Servis Filmsetting Limited, Manchester
Printed in Great Britain
by William Clowes & Sons Limited, Beccles, Suffolk
for the publishers
B T Batsford Limited, 4 Fitzhardinge Street, London W1H 0AH and
Charles T Branford Company, Newton Centre, Massachusetts

Contents

Acknowledgment

I would like to thank Thelma M. Nye of B. T. Batsford Limited for suggesting that I present the work I was undertaking with my students as a book. Without her inducement it is unlikely that this would have happened.

I would also like to express my gratitude to Constance Howard, ARCA, for her stimulation and help over the years. It is her enthusiasm that is largely responsible for my interest in thread as a creative medium.

I particularly wish to thank the photographers for their excellent visual presentation; A. G. Evans, BA, Senior Lecturer, Audio-Visual Centre, Ethel Wormald College of Education for figures 1, 2, 10, 17, 18, 19, 20, 21, 22, 24, 25, 28, 29, 30, 31, 35, 37, 38, 39, 41, 42, 43, 44, 59 and colour plate 2; J. Sidney Bailie, FRMS, ARPS, AIMBI for figure 13 and Tudor G. Williams, FRPS, AIIP, by courtesy of Liverpool Polytechnic, for all other photographs. Their co-operation and help is much appreciated.

To the students of the Ethel Wormald College of Education who have so willingly allowed me to reproduce photographs of their work, I am immensely grateful.

My special thanks to E. Bay Tidy, OBE, for her personal interest in this, and all my work.

Introduction

Throughout history, thread has been used for utilitarian purposes and to express ideas. From time to time, there has been evidence of man's desire to explore thread itself, for example, the fine sensitive fringing of the Chimu thread dolls dating back to the tenth century, and the knotting of thread for couching, to give textural interest, which was so popular during the reign of William and Mary. It is only in recent times, however, that it has been truly recognized that thread possesses qualities inimitable in other media.

The aim of this book is to consider the potential of thread as a creative medium. This can best be done by exploring and experiencing the very nature of thread. The appearance of new fibres is a constant impetus and challenge to the curious mind. Much can be learnt from the freshness of approach and the spontaneous response of the child, leading to a vitality so often yearned for by the inhibited adult.

The ideas presented are offered to stimulate an interest in thread and to encourage exploration. Much of the work can be attempted by beginners, and it is hoped that some of the concepts will be a springboard for further development by the more experienced.

The emphasis throughout is on concept rather than on technique. When the latter takes prominence, it becomes a hinderance to creative expression. For ease of reference, however, the work has been divided into sections according to the particular method employed.

Though the simplest thread offers unlimited scope for design development, no thread or technique should be regarded in isolation. Through the correlation and overlapping of ideas and methods, and an experimental approach, the possibilities become infinite. The emotional and intuitive reaction to thread should never be ignored. One would agree with John Ruskin that the best results in any art form can be achieved when 'the hand, the head and the heart of man go together'.

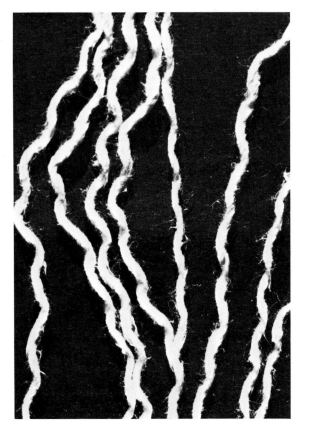 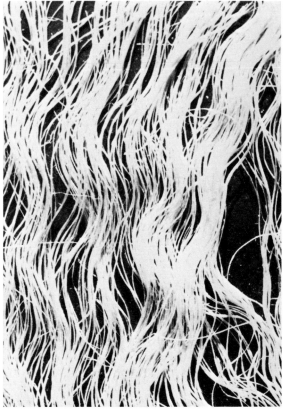

1 Sisal untwisted to show
single ply

2 Sisal untwisted into its
individual fibres

12

1 Threads

In order to express ideas through the medium of thread, it is essential to know the materials at one's disposal and be fully aware of their potential.

The term 'thread' is used to cover a wide range, including all types of string, rope, wool, cotton, silk, wire, raffia, chenille, and all threads made of man-made fibres, including nylon monofilament and plastic thread.

Threads already made up into material can also be used. Fabric, whether knitted, woven or bonded, can be cut into strips and used as threads. Nylon stockings or tights cut spirally give a continuous length which is ideal for weaving. The nylon, once cut, will roll back on itself, forming a narrow tube.

Plastic and metal pan scourers can be unravelled; the thread which is obtained will retain a high twist.

Vegetable bags can be cut into narrow strips to form a thin thread, or cut into wide strips and folded or rolled, giving body but retaining a delicate appearance. These can be couched or woven.

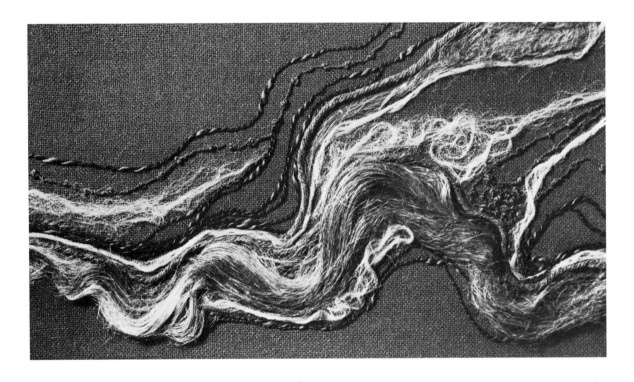

EXPLORATION OF THREADS

3 Random arrangement of
threads following flowing lines
of jute. The contrast can be
seen between the jute, knitting
wool and knotted yarn

Each thread has its own characteristics. It is only by handling and experimenting
that the possibilities and limitations of the threads can be discovered. One type of
string may be limp and pliable, another wiry and springy. Wool is generally soft,
fluffy and easy to handle. Some threads have more than one quality; raffia, when
plaited or knotted, can be strong and tough, but, cut lengthwise into thin strips,
it can give a very delicate effect (figure 5). It is only through the process of
investigation that such characteristics are revealed.

14

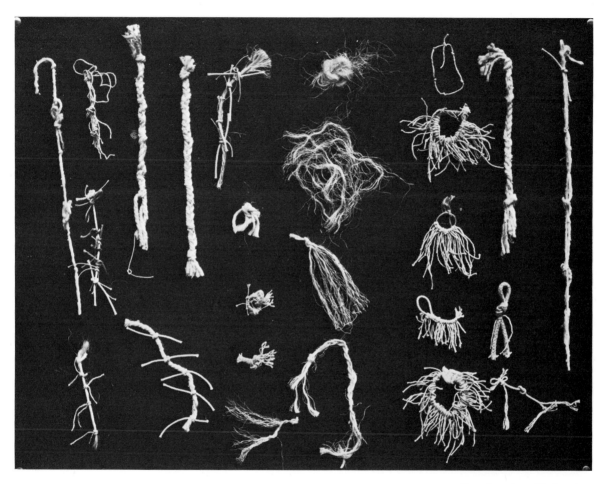

4   Experimenting with threads
by 5-year-old children at Teulon
Street Primary School, Liverpool

15

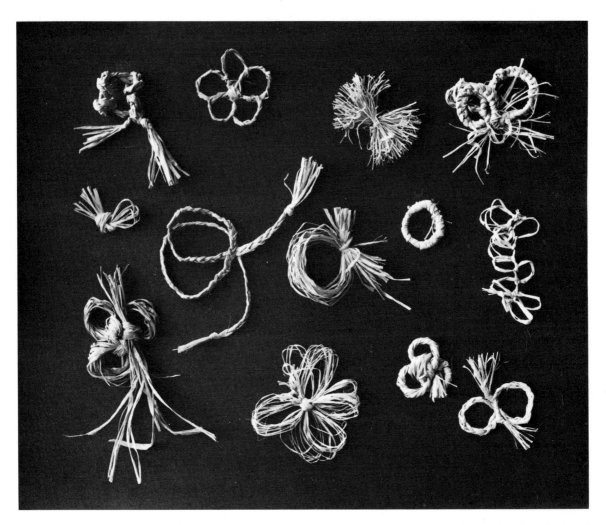

5 Exploring the properties of raffia

There is a wide range of interesting threads readily available, and yet the simpler the thread, the greater the scope for creativity. Simple threads may be constructed into many unusual forms by knotting, plaiting, coiling, looping and tufting. No tool other than the finger is needed for this. Other variations may be produced by using a crochet hook or knitting needles. A sturdier, more textural version of any thread can be obtained by casting on a number of stitches on a knitting needle of a suitable size, then casting off on the next row. This new form lends itself to crochet, plaiting or looping.

Multiple threads such as thick string or rope may be untwisted to give a single ply, and untwisted still further until one fibre is obtained (figures 1 and 2). These varied thicknesses of one basic thread provide sufficient contrast for working a collage, woven or embroidered panel or structure (figures 11 and 49). If desired, each separate ply or fibre could be reconstructed in the form of knitting, knotting, etc as mentioned above.

Great variety can be obtained from one thread alone. Using the same type of thread in its different forms ensures good material relationship in a design. It is a greater challenge and can be more rewarding to derive the maximum potential from one thread than to use a variety of complex threads.

This is not a limitation, however, that should be imposed on all work. Threads can be used to contrast with and complement each other (figure 3). For instance, a shiny thread may be needed to highlight work based on thread of a matt character; or a thread of a wiry nature may be necessary as a contrast to a soft, fluffy thread.

6 Relief in copper, gilt and
silver wire. The wire was
curved by drawing it over a
pencil

7 Thread drawn out of the
two-toned background fabric
gives a delicate line for contrast

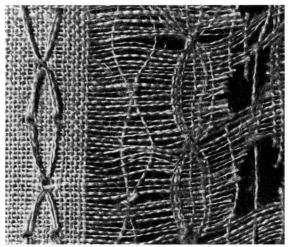

8 *(above left)* Onion bag threads were pushed together to make an interesting background. This could form the framework for embroidery or free weaving

9 *(above right)* Hessian background with threads drawn out. The remaining threads have been cut, pushed out of place and tied

10 *(right)* Threads have been drawn out of hessian background and re-inserted in another form

Being guided by the natural characteristics of the thread will lead to sound craftsmanship. Whilst design is of great importance, one is unlikely to achieve a successful piece of work without a sensitive understanding of the materials being used. The choice of threads is one of the most important aspects of design and a full knowledge of their potential will help to produce creative work.

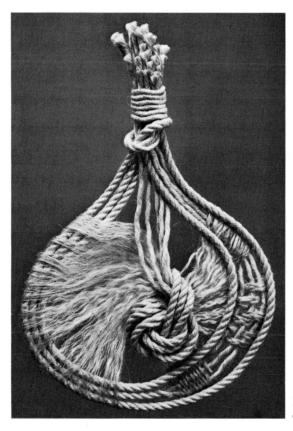

11 Rope structure by Beryl Platt. The strength and fineness of rope are contrasted

12 Experimenting with line by knitting, knotting, plaiting and looping thread. Cottons, wools and leather thonging were used. Thread drawn out of the hessian background was knitted and re-inserted to fill the spaces

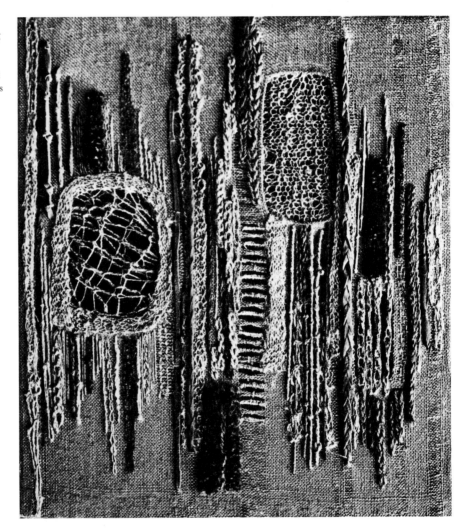

2 Texture

Concern with texture is now evident in most forms of art. Threads, however, offer the means of creating texture inimitable in other media, therefore their possibilities should be exploited to the full.

The original meaning of texture was a woven construction, but it is a term now accepted to denote surface quality, especially that which can be felt by touching.

We are surrounded by interesting and diverse texture. Nature is a rich source of inspiration, for instance the barks of trees (which in themselves offer a great variety), the surface of gourds, molluscs on rocks, fungi, mosses and lichen. A magnifying glass is very useful for revealing subtle textures that might otherwise go unnoticed.

The man-made world also displays a wide range of texture, from modern architecture to interior decoration. Figure 13 shows the rich cellular texture of building materials.

Weathering can enhance surfaces which in their original state might be of little interest. For example, the results of corrosion, or even scaling paint, could provide inspiration for experiments in texture (figure 14).

There are many ideas that can be derived from these sources, but as well as this, the nature of threads themselves can give sufficient stimulus to start off a series of rewarding activities.

13 *(left)* Building materials
showing cellular and
undulating textures

14 *(right)* Scaling paint

24

The two main groups of texture are rough and smooth, but these may vary in coarseness or fineness. Threads in themselves have a textural quality, some hairy, some smooth, some knobbly, some highly twisted. Simply gluing down areas of threads gives a wide range of textures. These threads can be mixed again in a number of ways to give greater variety.

By experimenting with the threads, the textural possibilities are enormous. Threads may be chopped and glued in a flat, curved or upright position; surfaces of knots may be formed and the knots may vary in size, shape and mass (figures 15 and 16).

Threads can also be coiled, plaited or undulated; looping and interlacing gives further variety (figures 22 to 26). In figure 25 mercerized cotton has been coiled round a pencil, stiffened (see chapter 3) then glued onto a background. Figure 26 shows another variation.

Texture may be created by the removal of thread as much as by the addition of it. Experiments can only be carried out with fairly loosely woven fabrics such as scrim, hessian, some furnishing fabrics and some woollen material. A simple method is to remove alternate threads from warp and weft. Many variations can be worked on this theme by removing different numbers of threads. This alters the entire character of the original fabric. The remaining threads can be pushed together so as to alternate tightly packed areas with open spaces, or they may be tied together regularly or irregularly (figures 9 and 10). The threads drawn out of the fabric can be reinserted by different methods such as looping or tufting. Groups of drawn-out threads can be plaited or knotted and then woven back into the loose channels. Contrasting threads may also be used. Figure 30 shows loosely spun silk woven into a textured hessian background.

15 *(left)* String chopped and
glued onto cardboard

16 *(right)* Lengths of string
knotted at intervals and glued

17 The single ply of packing
string gives a wavy effect.
Strands were glued onto thick
card

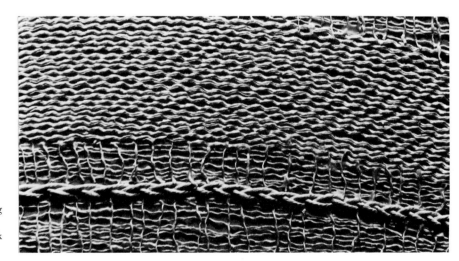

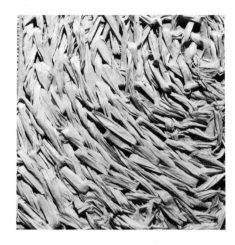

18 *(left)* Length of raffia loosely looped then glued in quadrant formation onto cardboard

19 *(right)* Raffia folded to give a chevron effect

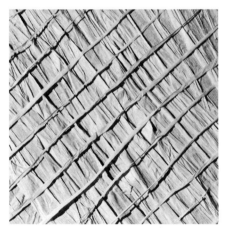

20 *(left)* Raffia opened out and glued diagonally onto strawboard. Narrow strips have been cut and glued in the opposite direction

21 *(right)* Raffia cut into short lengths, grouped and tied

22 Untwisted dish-cloth
cotton cut into short lengths,
coiled and glued onto
cardboard

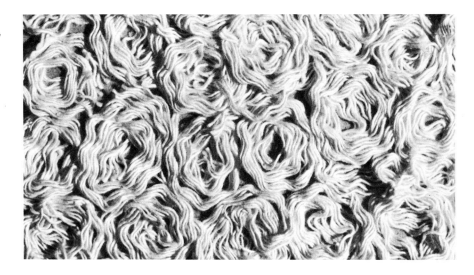

23 Lengths of twine part-
plaited, part-untwisted and
splayed. These were alternated
and glued onto cardboard

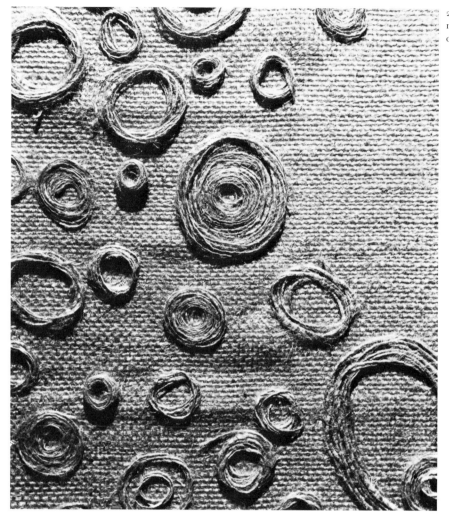

24　Threads drawn out of natural colour hessian were coiled and glued

25 Mercerized cotton coiled over a pencil, stiffened and glued, giving undulating texture

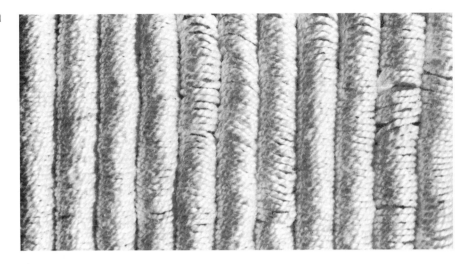

26 Mercerized cotton coiled, twisted, stiffened and glued

27 Iron grid structure suggests texture and tonal quality that could be achieved by drawing threads from fabric

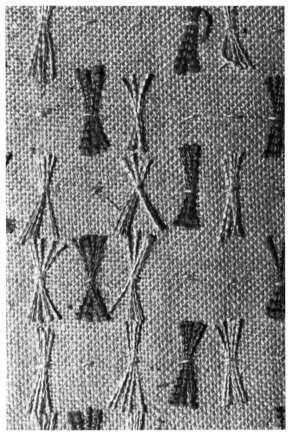

28 *(left)* Weft threads
of hessian cut and frayed

29 *(right)* Natural and
dark-brown threads drawn
from hessian, cut into short
lengths, grouped and stitched
onto natural hessian ground

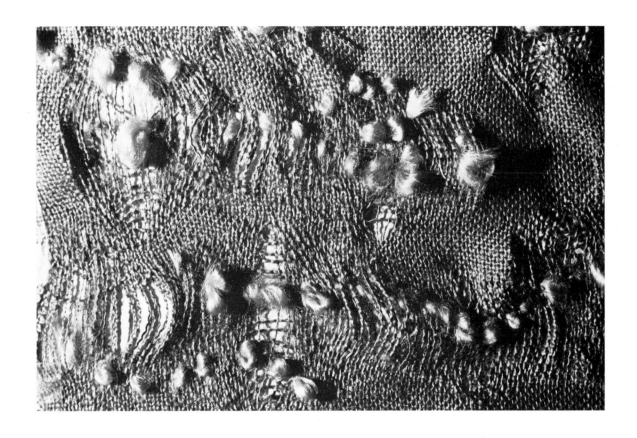

Plate 2 *(opposite)*   Panel in
straight stitch on canvas by
Margaret Robinson

30 *(above)*   Natural colour silk
thread darned into olive hessian
ground to replace drawn-out
threads

33

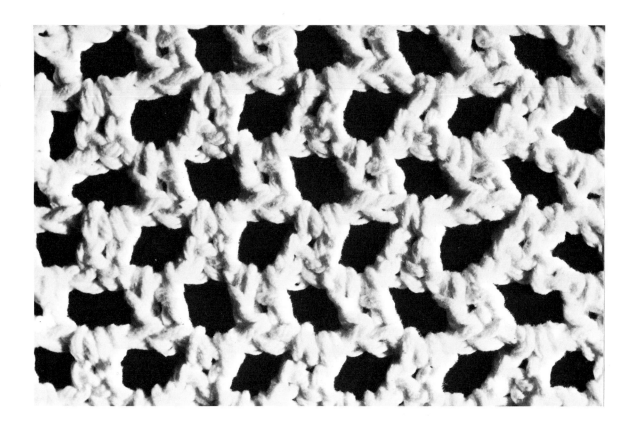

CROCHET, KNITTING, HOOKING AND WEAVING

If techniques other than gluing are used, the range of textures that can be obtained is limitless. Crochet and knitting, crafts which are generally employed in more functional ways, can be used most successfully in threadwork to add textural interest (figures 31 to 34).

31   Enlargement showing texture obtained by crochet

34

32　Plain and purl knitting giving looped effect. For each stitch of the plain row, the wool was wound twice round needle and forefinger of left hand

33　Knitted loops were cut

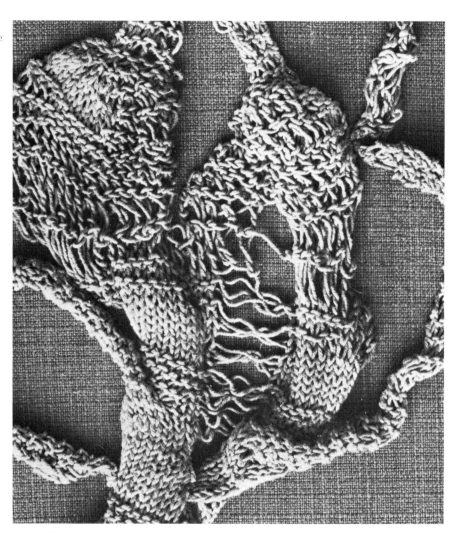

34 Detail showing textural quality of knitting. Use of large needles gives a looser effect in parts and dropping of stitches adds to textural interest

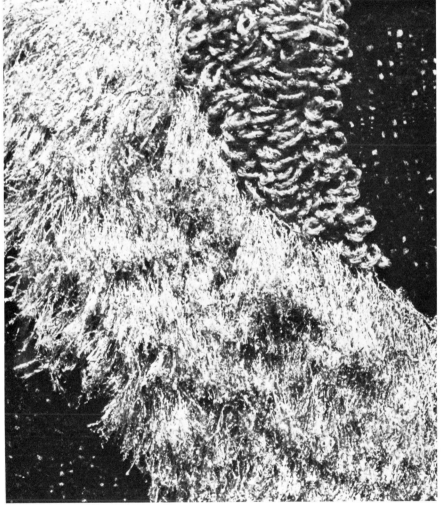

35 Wool and *Lurex*. Rug hooking technique was used on a loosely woven wool ground. Wool loops were left uncut. *Lurex* loops were cut for greater contrast

Rug-making techniques can also be used in this way (figures 35 and 39). The simplest type of rug hook for this kind of work is the punch hook. Wool or yarn is threaded through its tubular stem. Holding the fabric face downwards, the hook is pushed up and down through it in a forward movement. This forms a loop which remains when the hook is withdrawn. Some punch hooks can be adjusted to form a high or low pile. Sizes vary and it is possible to buy small ones suitable for fine embroidery thread. Loops can be left uncut, or cut to form tufts (figure 35). The result will vary greatly according to the type of thread used. Some threads stand rigidly, others fall gracefully. To prevent loops or tufts being pulled out, dab a small quantity of *Marvin Medium* and water solution on the back and leave it to dry.

Weaving is another craft which produces many different textures (figures 36 and 37). Simply varying the threads used for tabby weaving, which takes the form of darning, can be effective. Inserting knotted, looped or tufted threads alters the tactile and visual quality of the surface still further.

36 *(opposite above left)* Lengths of string looped fairly tightly, then woven to give a highly textured basket weave

37 *(opposite above right)* Double weave in raffia. Length of raffia wound round card. The raffia was then woven in one continuous length over back and front strands, leaving one side open for removal of card

38 *(opposite below)* Areas of raised chain band were stitched on the bars formed by the weft of the matt orange and red furnishing fabric. Red Perlita thread was used.

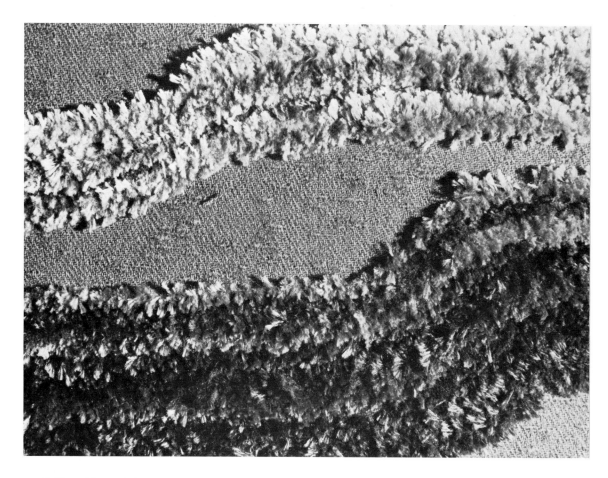

39 Tufting with stranded
cotton in shades of cinnamon
and brown on slub woollen
fabric in mid brown

In embroidery there is no end to the range of textures that can result from experimenting. One stitch worked in a variety of threads produces totally different results, eg French knots in a fine strand contrast greatly with the same stitch worked in rug wool. Different kinds of stitches can be combined to contrast with each other – flat stitches such as seeding with chunky ones such as knotted chain. It is not necessary to use a wide variety of stitches to achieve interesting work, and often the simpler stitches are more adaptable.

Machine embroidery offers much scope (figures 41 to 43). Different results can be obtained by varying the size and type of stitch, tension and direction of movement. If the lower tension is loosened, the thread will come up in small loops around the upper thread (figure 41). Movement can play an important part in determining the textural effect. Close circular movement (figure 43) gives a highly textural result; straight rows of similar stitching would form a more even surface.

In order to produce heavier lines of embroidery, a thicker thread may be used in the bobbin with fine machine cotton on top, for which a fairly loose tension is necessary (figure 44). The underside of the fabric becomes the right side. Experimenting with thread and tension will produce many different effects. Fine machine embroidery could also be used successfully with chunky hand embroidery.

At the exploratory stage the main aim should be the manipulation of thread with respect for its characteristics. An imaginative use of the materials will only come about by freely experimenting without concerning oneself about the end result.

41

41 Machine embroidery.
Variegated machine
embroidery thread in shades of
peach and brown was used on
peach-coloured cotton fabric.
Looping around the top thread
was caused by loose lower
tension

43

42 Zig-zag machine stitch in chestnut-brown machine embroidery cotton on sculpture scrim

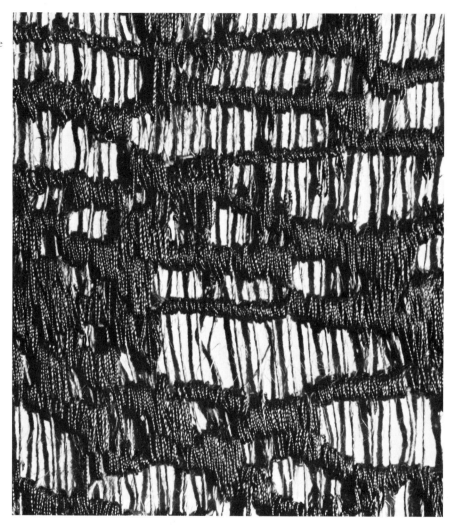

43 Machine embroidery in variegated black and red machine embroidery cotton on red *Viyella*. Very loose lower tension and close circular movement, with rapid transfer from unit to unit for continuity

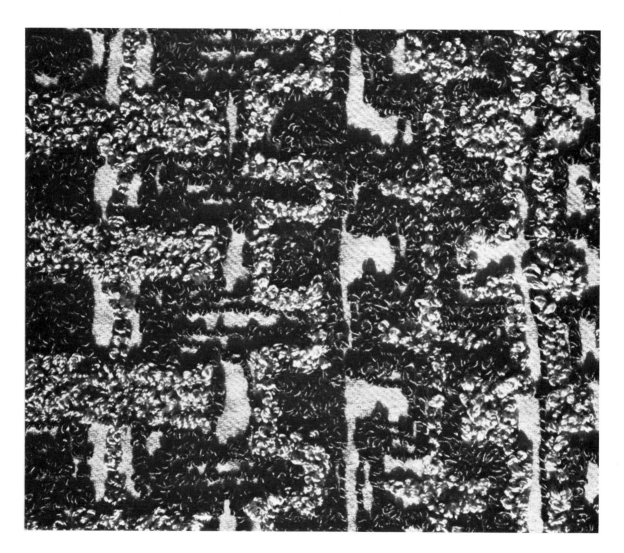

Texture adds vitality to a piece of work and a design in a single colour relies upon it for much of its interest. Too much variety, however, can be confusing, especially if several colours are used.

As suggested for the exploration of threads, a panel could be executed very successfully in only one type of thread, varying texture and also the thickness and nature of line. An alternative would be to use one colour throughout, but with different types of thread, eg rough, smooth, dull, shiny.

Texture creates colour variation and it is surprising how one thread can give a different colour or tonal effect depending on the form it takes. For instance, some nylon yarn appears dull in its original form, more lustrous when pulled apart and adopts a high sheen and depth of tone when tufted. The appearance of the threads used will change according to how the light falls on their surface.

Rough or undulating textures give greater variety of tone because the unevenness of the surface causes shadow and highlight. When producing any work in threads one should constantly bear in mind the interdependence of texture, colour and light.

44 *(opposite)* Machine embroidery on orange *Viyella* using orange and purple sylko perlé on the spool. Loose lower tension

45 Thread construction.
Detail of figure 53

Plate 3 *(opposite)* Woven
hanging by Dorothy Sanders,
using fishing line warp. For
subtle colour wool was dyed

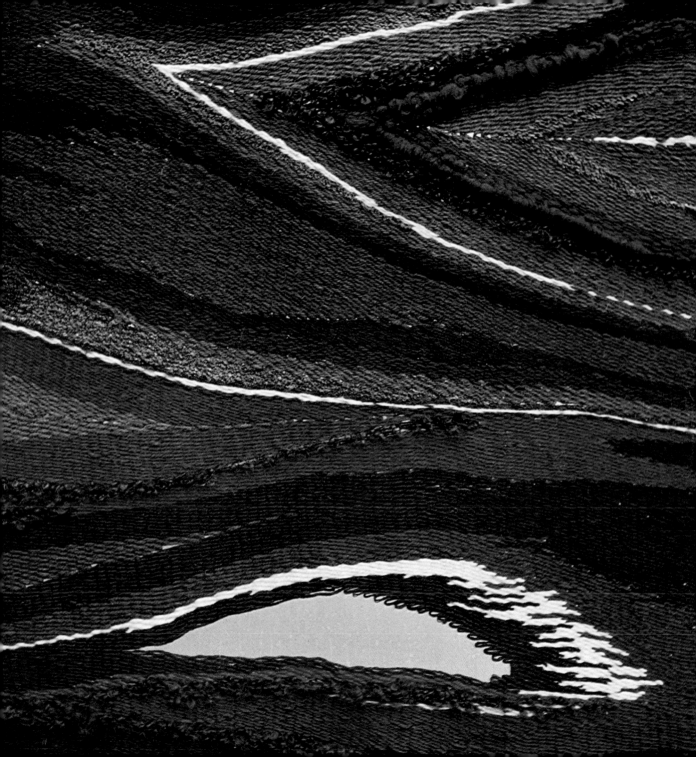

3 Collage, constructions and stitchery

SELECTION OF THREADS

The exploratory work already covered leads to the understanding of the particular qualities of each thread. This, however, must only be regarded as a means to an end. Though what goes on at the investigative phase is a most valuable process, it is of no real worth unless it is utilized to express a creative idea.

Having discovered the qualities and potentialities of each thread, it is now up to the individual to explore still further and find the right threads with which to express an idea. A combination of threads may be the answer, or perhaps one type of thread used to its maximum potential. The choice of thread is highly personal and it is through the materials selected that ideas and feelings can be expressed.

49

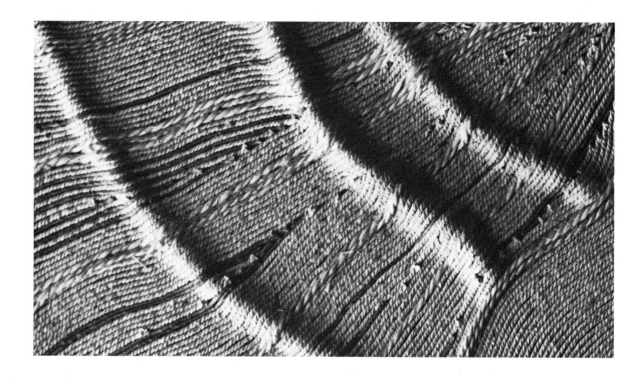

COLLAGE

The word 'collage', derived from the French verb 'coller', means to stick or glue.

One of the simplest and possibly quickest ways of applying thread to a background is gluing. Its speed allows for results to be achieved before enthusiasm wanes. It also provides an opportunity for those who are not acquainted with stitches to use thread as an expressive medium. Furthermore, it allows threads to be attached to backgrounds such as strawboard, hardboard, metal and slate where stitching could not be used.

46 String collage by Stella Ansell. Rope glued onto the card base underneath the string gives the undulating effect

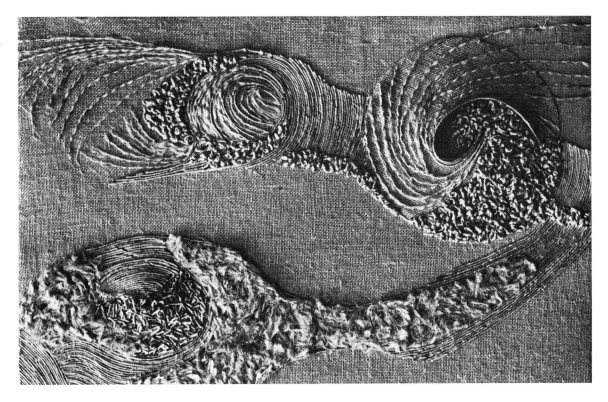

47 Collage by Joan Cotterill.
Brown packing string on a
cardboard base covered with
fine tailor's canvas. Some areas
were padded with layers of felt
before covering with string or
fabric. Knotted, untwisted,
coiled, frayed and chopped
string gives textural interest

51

It is important to find the appropriate adhesive and a sample test is recommended. Work can be ruined by unsatisfactory gluing. The background as well as the threads must be borne in mind, as material reactions to adhesives will vary. If the adhesive is strong and suitable for the materials in question, only a small amount is needed. *Marvin Medium* and *Copydex* are excellent for this type of work.

If an intricate line is to be followed, the thread can be held in position by pins placed at intervals. Applying the adhesive sparingly to the thread with the point of a needle will prevent surplus adhesive showing. It is advisable to remove the pins before the glue is completely dry otherwise they may be difficult to take out. When working on a surface that cannot be penetrated by pins, lines of thread may be held in position by small, flat weights placed at intervals along their length. The weights can be removed one by one as the gluing proceeds. One or more types of thread may be employed and the result can be flat or in relief.

Figures 46 to 51 show the use of a limited range of threads. It is interesting to note the different appearance of string in long, straight lengths to the same string tightly knotted (figure 48).

Figure 51 is executed mainly in one type of string and shows chopping, knotting, fraying, looping and plaiting. The coiled area together with the criss-cross surface give a three-dimensional quality to the work.

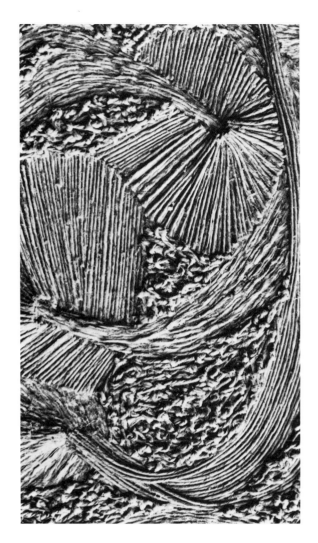

53

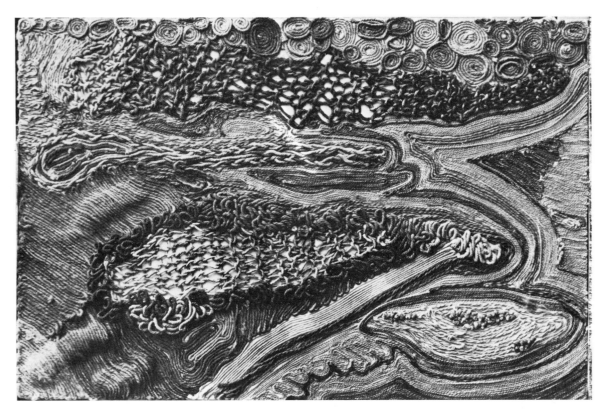

50 Collage by Enid Griffin,
in off-white string and fine
weaving cotton. Some threads
dyed in shades of brown and
purple. Small areas slightly
padded with sisal. Knitting,
looping, plaiting and knotting
give textural interest

54

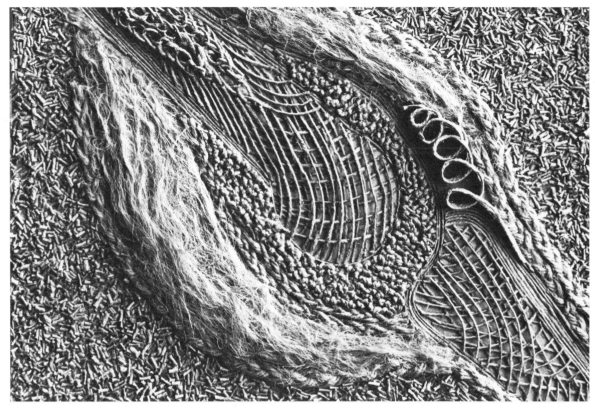

51 Collage by Joan Cotterill.
To cover an area with chopped
string, apply adhesive to the
base, drop the string into
position and press lightly. For
criss-cross and coiled sections,
apply adhesive sparingly to
each thread

55

52 Detail of collage by Jean Clarkson, showing use of a variety of threads and padded areas of knitting

Three-dimensional work in thread is becoming increasingly popular. A wood, metal or wire framework can be constructed and the thread worked over this basic structure.

There is also much scope for threadwork in relief without any structural support. If the thread is strong and sturdy it will need little support. However, for more delicate work where fine thread such as sewing cotton, soft thread such as wool or certain kinds of string are employed, it is necessary to work over a mould and afterwards stiffen the threadwork. Dependent on the design, the thread relief can be worked in one with the background threadwork as a continuous process (figure 54), or it may be necessary to construct it independently and attach it in its appropriate position afterwards.

If the mould used has a porous surface, it is advisable to smear it with vaseline or cover it with thin polythene (polyethylene) before beginning. This will prevent the thread from sticking to the surface when the stiffener is applied. Plastic and glass are ideal surfaces over which to work the constructions as they repel the stiffener, consequently there is no difficulty in removing the thread form.

The simplest method is to work the thread freely in criss-cross manner over the mould (figures 53 to 55). When the construction is completed, lightly sponge it with the appropriate stiffening solution and leave it to dry. For stiffening a relief made of sewing thread (figure 53), a solution of sugar and water can be used. Heat four tablespoonfuls of sugar in 250 ml ($\frac{1}{2}$ pt) of water until dissolved. When applied, it adds body to the thread and gives a slightly frosted effect.

For more durable results and where a thicker thread is used, a solution of *Marvin Medium* and water is recommended. Place one tablespoonful of *Marvin Medium* in a pint of cold water and mix thoroughly. Whichever stiffener is used, it is advisable to test the solution for strength, as threads will vary in their reaction, and with some threads it may be necessary to apply two or three coats.

57

Figure 53 was worked over a cone made of manilla card. Fine thread was wound round it in a criss-cross manner and lightly stitched at intervals to the outer edge of the cone. When the desired mesh quality had been achieved, the work was sponged with sugar solution and left to dry. The card was carefully cut away from the stitches and the cone removed, leaving the rigid form.

Figure 54 was constructed over an inflated balloon. The balloon was attached by *Sellotape* (*Scotch Tape*) onto the underside of a wooden framework, into which nails had been hammered at frequent intervals. The thread was wound round the nails and over the balloon, covering half its surface only to allow for the eventual removal of the balloon. To make the threads easier to control and place in position over the curved surface, they were first dipped in *Marvin Medium* solution. When the construction was completed, the entire surface was sponged with the solution and left to dry before the *Sellotape* (*Scotch Tape*) was removed to release the balloon.

Figure 55. The relief in the centre was worked separately over a plastic bowl and afterwards glued to the string collage.

These relief forms offer extensive possibilities. A mixture of threads may be used and a more textured line and varied background aimed for if desired. The constructions can exist in their own right or form part of other thread panels.

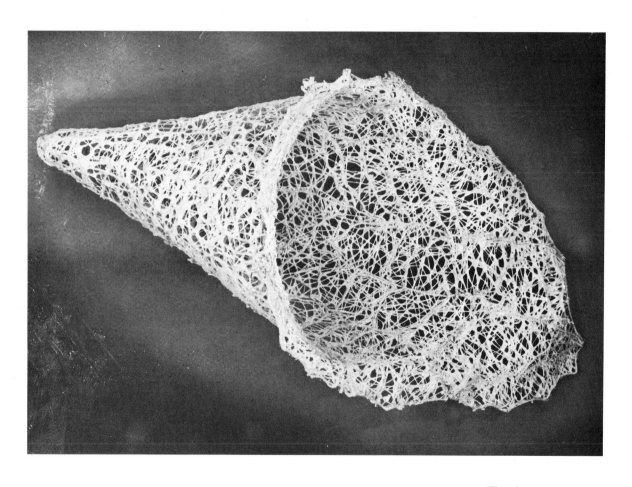

53 Thread construction by
Kathleen Hartley. The fine
thread was worked over a
manilla mould

54 Section of thread
construction by Michael
Bernard. This was worked over
an inflated balloon

55   Detail of collage and
construction by Kathleen
Hartley. The domed centre was
worked over a plastic bowl.
Natural colour twine formed
the background. Sisal was dyed
orange and brown. Untwisting
it after dyeing gave variegated
effect

56 Panel by Margaret Roberts. This was inspired by the fringing of two-toned furnishing fabric. Strips of fabric were cut and fringed, some strips showing the cerise rayon warp and some the blue cotton weft fringe. Unfringed edges were turned under and inconspicuous running stitches held these in place. Areas were padded with *Terylene* wadding before being covered. Fringed and undulating areas were lightly sprayed with fixative for stiffening and retention of line and shape

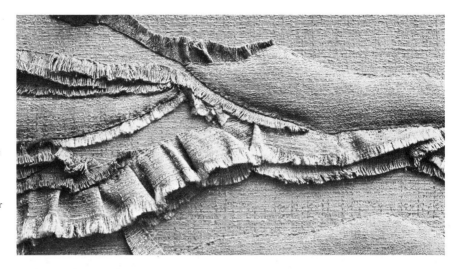

57 Panel by Doris Wood-Glover. Strips of natural colour hessian cut and partly fringed. These were coiled round card shapes and the ends glued. Each unit was stiffened before gluing onto the base of cardboard covered with hessian

62

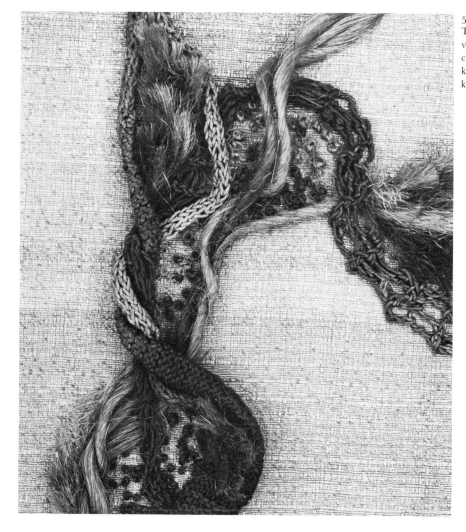

58 Panel by Enid Griffin. This was inspired by creeping vine and worked in knitting, couching, tufting and French knots. Tufting and tubular knitting give depth

59   Pattern by Marianne
McDonough developed from
experimenting with size and
shape of unit in straight stitch.
Hessian formed the background
and *Anchor* soft embroidery
cotton was used for the stitches

Thread collage, despite its advantages has certain limitations. Sometimes greater variety of line and texture may be necessary; this can be achieved by the use of hand and machine stitches.

It is not intended to cover the enormous number of stitches that can be used. The inexperienced need not be inhibited by lack of knowledge of stitchery or techniques. However, the method of experimenting with simple stitches can equally be applied to more complicated ones.

Everyone is capable of pushing a needle in and out of fabric. The variations achieved by this simple process are unlimited and give ample scope for the expression of ideas. The end result can be flat and smooth, knobbly, looped or tufted.

Couching is one of the simplest stitching methods of attaching thread onto a background (figure 64). The thread to be attached is held in position by another thread. The thread used for couching may be fine and unobtrusive, or thick and bold. As the thread to be couched does not have to pass through the fabric, it can be highly textural in character.

With couching, the main concern is with surface quality rather than the type of stitch employed, and threads can be selected and created accordingly. Knotted threads give a knobbly surface; tufts tied onto the basic thread would give either a smooth or shaggy appearance. Threads can also be looped and couched in position.

It is the constant awareness of the possibilities of threads at one's disposal that leads to creative results and not the number of stitches employed.

Plate 4 *(opposite)*   Panel by
Joan Cotterill. Domed circular
area was worked over fishing
line warp stitched in centrifugal
formation. Straight lines were
couched

60 Experimental work by Mair Morris. Detail showing illusion of movement and depth obtained by straight stitch. The background was of copper mesh and the thread used was a mercerized weaving cotton in ecru. Change of thread direction gives tonal variation

The straight stitch or running stitch allows for innumerable variations (figures 59 and 60). It will change its character according to the type of thread used, the size of the stitch, the background it is worked into and the direction it follows. It may be worked evenly or unevenly, and interesting effects can be produced simply by changing the size and direction of this stitch when filling an area on an

66

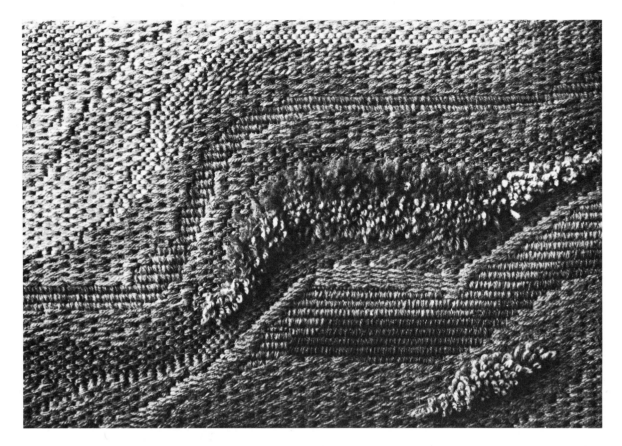

evenweave background such as canvas (figure 61). With running stitch, the nature of the thread remains evident throughout, whether it be highly twisted or smooth; often the character of the basic thread is lost when more complicated stitches are used.

61 Panel by Marianne McDonough. This was worked in wool in shades of purple and violet on canvas. Change in size and direction of straight stitch gives variety. Tufting was included for contrast

67

62   Panel by Mair Morris,
540 mm × 540 mm (1 ft 9 in. ×
1 ft 9 in.). Nylon thread used
throughout in shades of purple,
red and orange. Tufting gives a
textural and lustrous effect

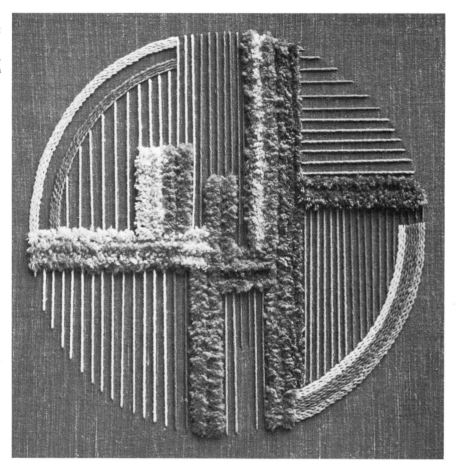

Figure 62 shows how three different results can be produced from one type of thread. The long straight stitch displays the thread in its natural form, the stem stitch or slanted stab stitch gives a chequered effect and the tufting makes a rich deep pile. Nylon knitting yarn with a matt surface was used; but when tufted this displayed a high sheen.

The simplest way of getting an even result when looping and tufting with needle and thread is to hold a pencil or plastic tube firmly on the surface of the fabric, bringing the thread out on one side of it and back in on the other for the required length. When the tube is removed, loops may be left intact or may be cut to give a tufted appearance. A tiny back stitch can be used to secure each stitch, or *Marvin Medium* applied as for rug hooking. Other more complicated methods of looping and tufting could be followed if desired.

63 *(overleaf left)* Detail of experimental work by Jenny Wright. Straight stitch, couching and looping in clover, maroon and aubergine tapestry wool on natural hessian background

64 *(overleaf right)* Section of panel by Margaret Robinson. White threads, some knotted, were couched by machine onto white organdie background

4 Weaving, dyeing and needleweaving

The techniques of weaving on a loom will not be dealt with here but the suggestions for experimentation with threads can be carried out equally well on a simple construction or an advanced loom. Before the invention of the loom, weaving was done with the fingers. Using this original technique can be challenging and offers endless scope for creative expression.

Weaving requires two sets of threads: a supporting or foundation set which is generally known as warp and another set of interlacing strands known as weft.

To support the warp a variety of devices may be used, eg card with serrated or notched edges and wooden frames of any shape. Warp threads may be wound round the frames or looped at one end and tied at the other. If these warp threads are to be held securely in position, nails may be hammered into the frame at regular or irregular intervals and the thread wound round them so as to form a taut basis for the weft.

Lampshade rings may also be used; it is easier to attach the warp threads if the rings are first bound or buttonholed (figure 73).

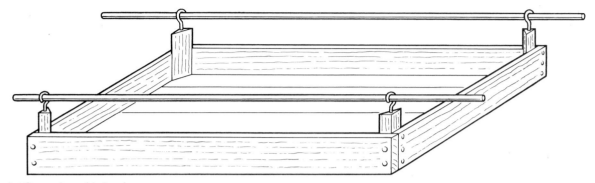

A   Orange box with dowels
fitted into cup hooks

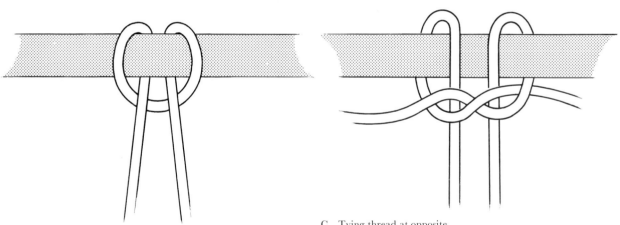

B   Attaching thread to top rod

C   Tying thread at opposite
end. Complete double knot

An excellent structure can be made from an old picture frame or an orange box, with a cup hook fixed at each corner to support rods such as dowelling, metal or glass, or bamboo cane. The looping and tying method may be adopted for attaching the warp. When the weaving is completed, the cup hooks can be swivelled outwards to release the rods. The work is then ready for hanging. The rod at the bottom may be left in place, or removed and the remaining length of warp threads fringed, plaited or knotted.

Supple tree branches bent so that the two ends are brought together and then tied make a good framework. Forks of branches may also be used (figure 65). These can give an interesting and varied outline, challenging one to think of new shapes and leading one away from the more usual geometric boundaries.

Depending on the type of basic structure, the warp threads may be spaced evenly or unevenly and may travel in one or many directions. Their main purpose is to provide a framework for the weft threads which can be interlaced regularly or irregularly, looped or tufted.

As the foundation thread does not have to pass through the eye of a heddle, the device by which threads are raised or lowered on a loom, its thickness need not be considered, provided it is strong. In order to add interest, the foundation (or warp) threads used in one piece of work may vary in character, eg smooth threads may be combined with knotted or tufted threads. Transparent threads such as nylon monofilament, fishing line or cellophane may be used for the warp if the emphasis is to be on the weft threads.

The weft threads may be inserted with the fingers, or with a blunt needle or bodkin.

65   Tree branch with two ends tied together provided good tension for silk warp threads. Weft consisted of highly twisted silk, cotton sliver and artificial raffia

66 *(opposite left)*   Detail, showing the use of looped and knotted wool and rayon, untwisted nylon and fringed strips of fabric in orange, crimson and purple

67 *(opposite centre)*   Weaving by Enid Griffin. Free use of dyed sisal weft contrasts with the more even tabby weave in cotton. Irregular chain stitch was used to form the band appearing across the centre

68 *(opposite right)*   Panel by Jean Clarkson. Knitting wool, nylon and cotton threads in shades of red were the main threads used in this work. Strips of fabric and cut vegetable bags were used for tonal and textural effect

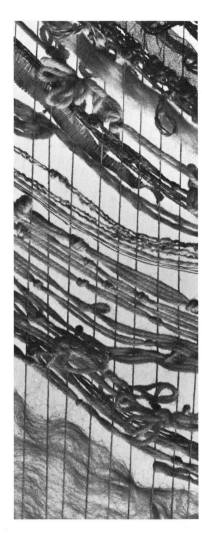

75

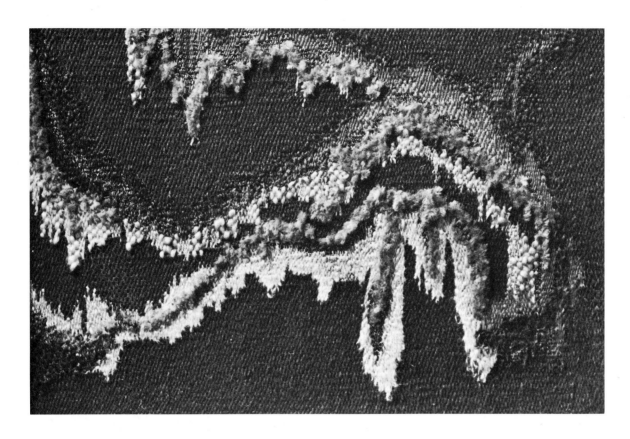

69 Free weaving by Joan Cotterill, using plain and textured wool and chenille in shades of mushroom, flame and yellow. Bronze *Lurex* used to highlight certain areas

As with other methods of thread design one type of thread could be used throughout in its different forms, or a variety of threads may be selected, contrasting smooth with knobbly, shiny with dull, bulky with fine. Fabrics may be cut into strips and these used as weft.

In figure 73 fabric strips form smooth areas to contrast with the more shaggy appearance of wool.

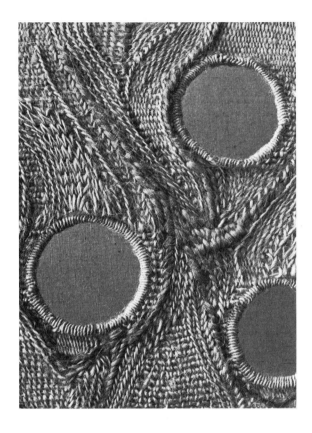

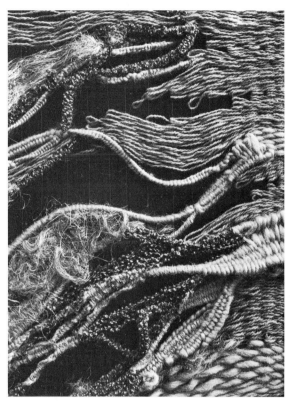

70 Panel by Dorothy Sanders, 110 cm × 80 cm (3 ft 7 in. × 2 ft 7½ in.). Binder twine created the lines and texture of this work. To retain the open spaces, button-holed lampshade rings were knotted into position during the warping process. Warp threads were then inserted into the button-hole stitches

71 Detail of panel by Margaret Roberts. The warp is nylon which allows the emphasis to be on the diverse character of the weft threads. Wire bound with thread and then bent was used in certain areas to give a three-dimensional effect

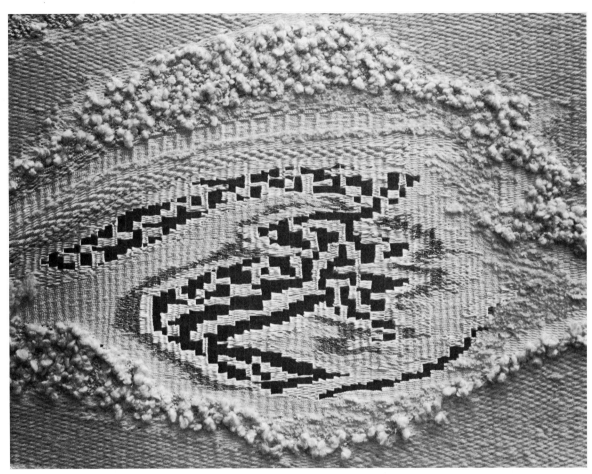

72 Section of panel by Joan Cotterill. Off-white threads were used. The dull, knobbly cotton contrasts with the delicate appearance of shimmering silk used for the needleweaving. The multi-toned fishing line warp is faintly visible

78

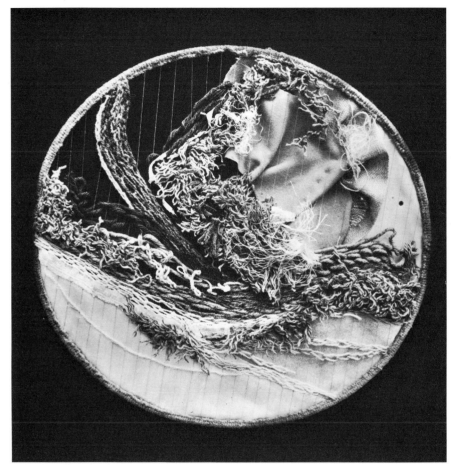

73 Weaving by Margaret Roberts, diameter 500 mm (1 ft 8 in.). Button-holed lampshade ring formed the framework of this weaving in shades of yellow, green and brown. Strips of hessian, rayon and woollen fabric used to contrast with the shaggy texture of untwisted yarn. Chain stitch used in parts

Experimenting with dyeing of thread can be most rewarding. Any household dye may be used, but to obtain the best results in a short time, it is better to halve the recommended quantity of water in order to strengthen the dye.

A good tonal range may be achieved by leaving some threads in the dye for a very short time, removing the rest in gradual stages until the last threads have reached dye saturation. This tonal range could be given to one thread alone by dipping the entire length in the dye, then gradually withdrawing it, so that the colour is pale at one end and deep at the other. Sections of a length of thread may be dipped in a variety of colours.

Different types of thread will absorb the dye at a different rate, and colour as well as tone can be influenced by the nature of the thread.

Highly twisted thread will not always be completely penetrated by the dye, therefore if it is dyed and then untwisted, a variegated effect may be the result. Figure 74 shows an interesting example of weaving and dyeing using white threads only, including cotton, wool, nylon, rayon and *Raffene*. The completed weaving was dipped in black dye. The wool absorbed the dye very quickly giving a dense black, the dye hardly penetrated the nylon, and other threads absorbed the colour in varying degrees. Experimenting in this way can suggest ideas for colour and tonal combinations. For developing this kind of work, more careful planning can be carried out by testing threads for colour absorbency.

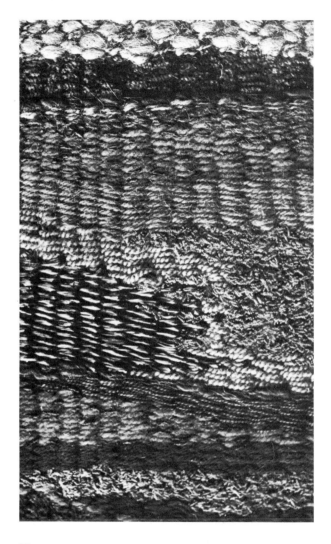

74   Weaving by Sheila Grey.
A variety of white threads were
used. The completed work was
dipped in black dye for a
subtle tonal effect

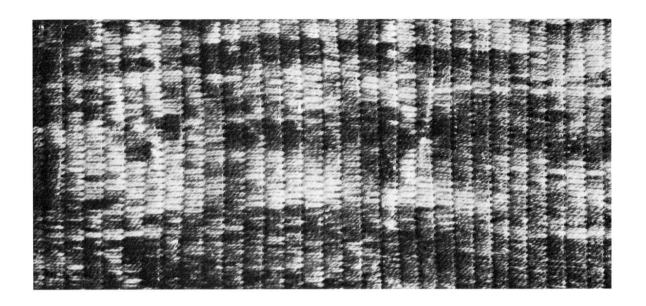

Ikat dyeing is basically the tie-dyeing of threads, and the technique probably
originated in India. It is a controlled method of producing pattern or design on
warp or weft threads in preparation for weaving.

Traditionally an Ikat stick was used. For controlled work, a stick is still recommended. This is a piece of wood about 50 mm (2 in.) square, and of the length
required for the warp or weft, dependent on which set of threads is to be dyed.
The stick is notched at intervals, the notches indicating the points at which the
threads are to be tied. A short length of dowelling is fixed across the top and
bottom of the stick, and the thread to be dyed is wound continuously round the
dowels from end to end, following the length of the stick.

82

It is customary to group the threads, and tie and bind them to the stick where the notches appear. If the Ikat stick is long, however, it presents difficulties, as a long dye trough would be required. It is easier if the threads are tightly bound together but not to the stick. This allows the threads to be slipped off the dowels when binding is completed, and a much smaller dyeing vessel is needed. Any type of thread may be used for binding, and the binding can extend over any length. If the area is solidly bound, dye will not penetrate, and the bound area retains its original colour when the binding is removed. By leaving gaps in the binding, a variegated effect is produced.

A freer method is to plan a design on paper and place this on a flat working surface. Lengths of thread are stretched over the design, leaving spaces wide enough for the design to show through. If areas of colour are blocked, they will show through much better. Threads can be held in position by *Sellotape* (*Scotch Tape*) at each end. Short lengths are recommended so that adjustments can be made when threads are grouped and bound according to the design.

If a streaked or dappled effect is wanted, threads can be knotted and dyed (figure 75). The knotting forms a certain amount of resist to the dye. Alternatively, threads can be knotted and the knots alone dipped in the dye.

When these threads are used for weaving, a nylon monofilament or cellophane warp or weft can be used successfully in conjunction with them (figure 75). The colourless nature of these would not interfere with the pattern or design of the dyed threads.

76 Weaving by Hilda Dodd. Silk fabric was tie-dyed in shades of blue, red and grey. This was cut into strips and woven

A length of fabric can be tie-dyed and then cut into strips. These strips can be used as weft, retaining the order in which they were cut. When woven, the result is a condensed form and slightly distorted outline of the original design. An inconspicuous warp is recommended (figure 76).

With the general overlapping of crafts it can be difficult to draw a line between free weaving and needleweaving. For the purpose of this book needleweaving incorporates weaving onto an already existing set of threads in a fabric, or onto stitches worked into a background fabric.

For needleweaving, a set of threads, generally the weft threads, are removed from a fabric, thus leaving a framework support for a new set of threads to be inserted. These new threads are woven or darned in and they can be plain or textured (figure 78). Weaving may be worked regularly over an even number of threads giving a chequered effect, or bar pattern (see centre of figure 72); or they may be worked quite freely (figures 77 to 79), depending on the result desired. The design may be carried out in self colour, or several colours may be introduced. In figure 79 threads of a similar character and colour to the background threads have been used, so the lace-like quality of the work becomes the dominant feature. Figure 77 shows an interesting example of a two-layered effect obtained by removing alternate threads from warp and weft. This allows weaving to proceed on two separate layers, each still attached to the background fabric.

For figure 80, a background of black velvet was stretched onto a frame so as to form a taut foundation for the warp. This consisted of long stitches in nylon monofilament placed vertically in such a way as to give a circular outline. Threads were dyed to yield subtle shades of black, grey, green and off-white, and these were regularly darned into the warp. The rows of dyed thread forming the weft were pushed so close together that the warp was concealed.

Needleweaving need not be worked on a flat surface. In figure 82 egg boxes were cut to form mounds and these were filled with *Terylene* wadding for support before being placed in position. Warp threads were worked over them in criss-cross manner to form a framework for the weft threads.

77 Needleweaving by
Dorothy Sanders. The
two-layered effect was obtained
by withdrawing alternate
threads from warp and weft
of peach-coloured hessian. This
automatically separated the
threads into two layers.
Threads drawn from the
background were used for
needleweaving the top layer,
and threads drawn from dark
brown hessian were used for
needleweaving the bottom
layer. Button-hole stitch was
worked along some of the
threads.

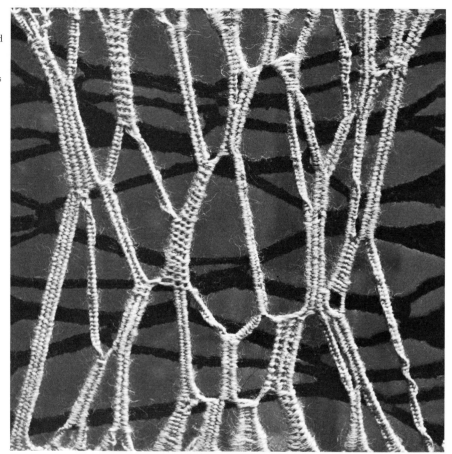

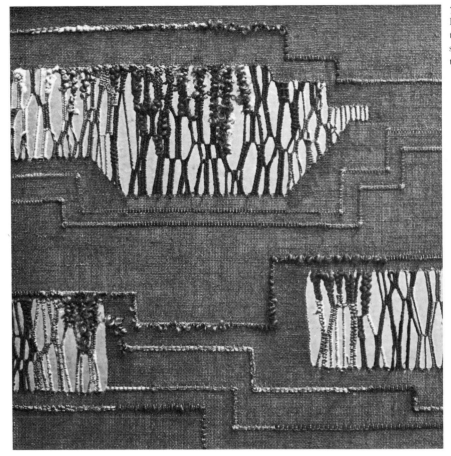

78 Section of panel by
Dorothy Sanders. Textured
thread adds interest. The
straight lines were darned into
the hessian background

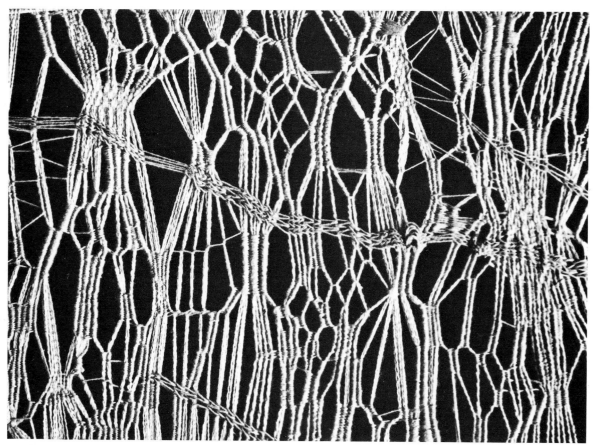

79 Needleweaving by Sheila
Grey. This was inspired by
rock veining. The background
was lime-green rayon
furnishing fabric. Mercerized
cotton thread of similar shade
was used and diagonal bands of
chain stitch introduced

88

80 Panel by Sheila Grey, diameter 550 mm (1 ft 9 in.). Nylon thread warp was stitched into black velvet background. Weft threads consisted of looped wool, plain and slub cotton, rayon and chenille in off-white, green, grey and black. Variegated effect was obtained by untwisting some threads after dyeing. Fine silver cord used to highlight certain areas

81 Needleweaving by
Dorothy Sanders. The use of
white cord gives the twisted
effect. Small nylon curtain
rings were button-holed with
white cotton

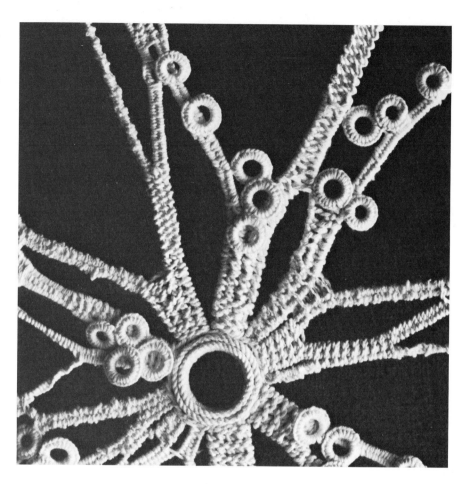

82 Detail of panel by
Dorothy Sanders, showing the
contrast that can be obtained
by needleweaving. *Courtelle*,
rayon, plain and slub cotton
threads in shades of turquoise
were used on ground of
straw-coloured woollen fabric
with turquoise flecks

91

Suppliers

Art Needlework Industries Ltd
7 St Michael's Mansions
Ship Street, Oxford
Various wools

J Hyslop Bathgate and Company
Victoria Works, Galashiels
Gimps, mohair, chenille, worsted

Craftsman's Mark Ltd
Trefnant, Denbigh
North Wales
Natural wools, fleece, warp flax

A K Graupner
Corner House, Valley Road
Bradford BD1 4AA
Inexpensive wools, yarn

Hugh Griffiths
Brookdale, Beckington
Bath, Somerset
Special yarns

Nathaniel Lloyd and Co Ltd
Tooley Street, London SE1
Cellophane – 25 mm (1 in.) wide

The Needlewoman Shop
146/148 Regent Street, London W1
*Wool, embroidery threads, nylon cords,
metal threads, string, macramé twine*

Mister Bosun's Locker
East Street, Chichester, Sussex
String, rope

Mersey Yarns
2 Stapland Road, Liverpool 14
Jute, flax, sisal, black macramé twine

Texere Yarns
9 Peckover Street
Bradford BD1 5BD
Bouclé, mohair loop, fancy yarns

Weavers' Shop
Royal Wilton Carpet Factory
Wilton, Wiltshire
Rug wools 6 ply and 2 ply, warp twine

Various types of yarns, threads, etc

Appleton Brothers of London
West Main Road, Little Compton
Rhode Island 02837

American Crewel Studio
Box 553 Westfield
New Jersey 07091

American Thread Corporation
90 Park Avenue, New York

Bucky King Embroideries Unlimited
121 South Drive
Pittsburgh, Pennsylvania 15238

The Needle's Point Studio
7013 Duncraig Court, McLean
Virginia 22101

Yarn Bazaar
Yarncrafts Limited
3146 M Street
North West Washington DC